Copyright © 2023 by S. J. Matthews (Author)

This book is protected by copyright law and is intended solely for personal use. Reproduction, distribution, or any other form of use requires the written permission of the author. The information presented in this book is for educational and entertainment purposes only, and while every effort has been made to ensure its accuracy and completeness, no guarantees are made. The author is not providing legal, financial, medical, or professional advice, and readers should consult with a licensed professional before implementing any of the techniques discussed in this book. The content in this book has been sourced from various reliable sources, but readers should exercise their own judgment when using this information. The author is not responsible for any losses, direct or indirect, that may occur from the use of this book, including but not limited to errors, omissions, or inaccuracies.

We hope this book has been informative and helpful on your journey to understanding and celebrating older adults. Thank you for your interest and support!

Title: The Evolution of Digital Gold
Subtitle: Examining the Growth and Potential of Bitcoin

Series: Decoding Satoshi's White Paper: A Three-Part Exploration of Bitcoin's Origins and Impact
By S. J. Matthews

"Bitcoin is a remarkable cryptographic achievement and the ability to create something that is not duplicable in the digital world has enormous value."
Eric Schmidt, former CEO of Google

"Bitcoin is the beginning of something great: a currency without a government, something necessary and imperative."
Nassim Taleb, author and economist

"The Bitcoin white paper is one of the most important innovations of our time, and it has the potential to change the way we think about money and finance forever."
Marc Andreessen, co-founder of Netscape and venture capitalist

"Satoshi's white paper on Bitcoin represents one of the most profound technological breakthroughs of our time. It's a blueprint for a new financial system that can be trusted, secure, and accessible to all."
Wences Casares, CEO of Xapo

"The Bitcoin white paper is a revolutionary piece of technology that has the potential to disrupt traditional financial systems and change the way we interact with money."

Andreas Antonopoulos, author and Bitcoin educator

Table of Contents

Introduction 7
Overview of the Bitcoin system and its components 7
Explanation of how transactions work in the system 9
Discussion of the role of miners in the system 11

Chapter 1: Creating Bitcoin Transactions 14
The process of creating a transaction 14
The importance of digital signatures in the process 17
The role of inputs and outputs in a transaction 19

Chapter 2: Validating Bitcoin Transactions 22
The role of nodes in validating transactions 22
The concept of a mempool and how it works 24
The importance of transaction fees in the validation process 27

Chapter 3: Mining Bitcoin Transactions 30
The role of miners in the system 30
The process of mining and creating new blocks 33
The concept of the block reward and its significance 36

Chapter 4: Securing the Bitcoin Network 39
The importance of network security in the Bitcoin system 39
The role of cryptographic protocols in securing the system 42

The potential threats to the system and how they can be mitigated 45

Chapter 5: The Lightning Network 48
Overview of the Lightning Network 48
The benefits and drawbacks of using the Lightning Network 52
The potential for the Lightning Network to solve Bitcoin's scalability challenges 55

Conclusion 58
The mechanics of Bitcoin transactions and how they contribute to the overall functioning of the system 58
The challenges facing the Bitcoin system and potential solutions, such as the Lightning Network 61
The potential for further developments in the Bitcoin system to improve transaction speed and scalability 64

Key Terms and Definitions 67
Supporting Materials 69
Bitcoin Whitepaper 69
Potential References 71

Introduction

Overview of the Bitcoin system and its components

The introduction is an essential part of any book as it sets the tone and provides a roadmap for the readers to understand what to expect from the book. In the context of this book, "The Evolution of Digital Gold," the introduction aims to provide the readers with a comprehensive overview of the Bitcoin system and its various components.

Bitcoin is a decentralized digital currency that operates on a peer-to-peer network. Its design is based on cryptographic protocols that secure the system, making it resistant to fraud and tampering. To understand how Bitcoin works, it is necessary to break it down into its components.

First and foremost, Bitcoin is a digital asset that can be bought, sold, or traded. It is stored in a digital wallet, which can be accessed via a private key. The wallet stores the user's Bitcoin address, which is a unique identifier used to send and receive transactions.

Bitcoin transactions are broadcast to the network, where they are verified by nodes. Nodes are computers that run the Bitcoin software, and their primary function is to verify and store transactions on the blockchain. The blockchain is a public ledger that records all transactions made on the Bitcoin network.

Miners are an essential component of the Bitcoin system. Their role is to validate transactions by solving complex mathematical problems. The mining process requires significant computational power, and as a reward for their efforts, miners receive newly minted bitcoins and transaction fees.

The Bitcoin system is designed to have a finite supply of 21 million bitcoins, of which over 18 million have already been mined. The remaining bitcoins will be mined over the next few decades until the total supply is reached.

Despite the growing popularity of Bitcoin, the system still faces several challenges. For example, the transaction speed is relatively slow, and the system can only process a limited number of transactions per second. This limitation has led to scalability issues, making it difficult for Bitcoin to compete with traditional payment systems.

The introduction concludes by highlighting the significance of understanding the Bitcoin system and its components. It sets the stage for the subsequent chapters of the book, which delve deeper into the mechanics of Bitcoin transactions and how they contribute to the overall functioning of the system.

Explanation of how transactions work in the system

Bitcoin is a decentralized digital currency that operates on a peer-to-peer network. Transactions on the Bitcoin network are the backbone of the system, allowing users to send and receive Bitcoin from one another. In this section, we will provide an overview of how transactions work in the Bitcoin system.

Bitcoin transactions are essentially transfers of value between two parties on the network. Each transaction is recorded on a public ledger called the blockchain, which is maintained by a network of nodes.

To initiate a transaction, a user must create a transaction request and broadcast it to the Bitcoin network. This request includes the sender's public key, the amount of Bitcoin being transferred, and the recipient's public key. Once the request is broadcast, it is picked up by nodes on the network who validate and verify the transaction.

Nodes on the network validate transactions by verifying that the sender has sufficient funds to complete the transaction and that the transaction conforms to the rules of the Bitcoin system. These rules include the requirement that transactions must be digitally signed using the sender's private key, and that each transaction must reference a previous transaction as input.

Once a transaction has been validated, it is added to the mempool, which is a pool of unconfirmed transactions waiting to be added to a block on the blockchain. Miners on the network are responsible for creating new blocks on the blockchain, and they do so by selecting a group of transactions from the mempool and adding them to a new block.

As miners create new blocks, they compete with one another to solve a complex mathematical puzzle, with the first miner to solve the puzzle being rewarded with new Bitcoin. Once a block has been created, it is added to the blockchain, and the transactions it contains are considered confirmed.

Overall, Bitcoin transactions work by allowing users to transfer value between one another on a decentralized network. Transactions are validated and verified by nodes on the network, and new transactions are added to the blockchain by miners who compete to solve complex mathematical puzzles. The end result is a fast, secure, and decentralized system for transferring value without the need for intermediaries.

Discussion of the role of miners in the system

In the Bitcoin system, miners play a crucial role in maintaining the integrity and security of the network. In this section, we will discuss the role of miners in the Bitcoin system in detail.

To begin with, miners are responsible for verifying and processing transactions in the Bitcoin network. When a user initiates a Bitcoin transaction, it is broadcasted to the network and added to a pool of unconfirmed transactions called the mempool. Miners select transactions from the mempool and include them in a new block that they add to the blockchain.

The process of creating a new block involves solving a complex mathematical puzzle that requires significant computational power. Miners compete with each other to solve this puzzle, and the first miner to solve it is rewarded with a set amount of newly minted bitcoins, as well as any transaction fees associated with the transactions included in the block.

The process of mining not only helps to process transactions but also plays a critical role in maintaining the security of the network. Each block that is added to the blockchain contains a unique cryptographic hash, which is a digital signature that verifies the integrity of the block. The hash of each block also includes the hash of the previous block in the chain, creating an immutable and tamper-proof ledger.

If a miner tries to modify a transaction in a block, it would change the hash of that block and all subsequent blocks in the chain. This would be detected by other nodes in the network, and the modified block would be rejected as invalid. Therefore, the more miners there are in the network, the more secure the network becomes, as it becomes increasingly difficult for any one miner to control the majority of the network's computing power.

In addition to processing transactions and maintaining network security, miners also play a role in determining the monetary policy of the Bitcoin system. The block reward that miners receive for adding a new block to the chain is programmed to decrease over time, with the goal of eventually reaching a total supply of 21 million bitcoins. As the block reward decreases, transaction fees will become an increasingly important source of revenue for miners.

Overall, the role of miners in the Bitcoin system is critical to its functioning and security. Without miners, the network would be vulnerable to attacks and would not be able to process transactions in a timely manner. As such, the Bitcoin system relies heavily on the incentives provided to miners to encourage their participation and investment in the network.

Chapter 1: Creating Bitcoin Transactions
The process of creating a transaction

The process of creating a Bitcoin transaction is a crucial aspect of the Bitcoin system, as it determines how the ownership of bitcoins is transferred from one user to another. In this chapter, we will delve into the details of how Bitcoin transactions are created.

To begin with, it is important to understand that Bitcoin transactions are not created by individual users, but rather by their Bitcoin wallets. Each Bitcoin wallet has a private key that is used to sign transactions and prove ownership of the bitcoins being transferred. When a user initiates a transaction, their wallet creates a digital message that contains the details of the transaction, including the recipient's address, the amount of bitcoins being transferred, and the fee that will be paid to miners for validating the transaction.

Once the transaction message is created, it is broadcast to the Bitcoin network, where it is picked up by nodes and added to a pool of unconfirmed transactions called the mempool. At this point, the transaction is considered pending, as it has not yet been validated by miners and added to the blockchain.

To ensure that the transaction is valid and can be added to the blockchain, it must be digitally signed by the sender's private key. This process involves using complex cryptographic algorithms to generate a unique signature that can be verified by anyone using the sender's public key. Once the transaction is signed, it is ready to be validated by miners.

It is worth noting that Bitcoin transactions can have multiple inputs and outputs, allowing users to send and receive bitcoins to and from multiple addresses in a single transaction. Each input represents bitcoins that are being spent, while each output represents the address to which the bitcoins are being sent. Transactions can also include additional data, known as a transaction comment, which can be used to include messages or notes about the transaction.

In order to prevent double-spending, where a user tries to spend the same bitcoins more than once, each input in a transaction must reference a previous transaction output. This ensures that the bitcoins being spent have not already been spent in another transaction.

Overall, the process of creating a Bitcoin transaction is a complex but essential aspect of the Bitcoin system. By understanding how transactions are created and signed, users can ensure the secure transfer of their bitcoins while also contributing to the overall security and functionality of the Bitcoin network.

The importance of digital signatures in the process

Digital signatures are a crucial component of the Bitcoin system, as they ensure the integrity and authenticity of transactions. In this section, we will explore the importance of digital signatures in the process of creating Bitcoin transactions.

A digital signature is a mathematical algorithm used to verify the authenticity of a message or document. In the case of Bitcoin, a digital signature is used to verify the ownership of a specific Bitcoin address and to authorize a transaction. Digital signatures are based on public-key cryptography, which uses a pair of keys, a public key, and a private key. The private key is used to sign the transaction, while the public key is used to verify the signature.

The process of creating a digital signature for a Bitcoin transaction involves several steps. First, the user creates a transaction by specifying the inputs, outputs, and the amount to be transferred. The user then generates a hash of the transaction, which is a unique identifier for the transaction. Next, the user signs the hash using their private key. This generates a digital signature that is specific to the transaction and the user's private key.

Once the digital signature has been generated, it is attached to the transaction and broadcast to the Bitcoin network. Nodes on the network then verify the transaction by checking that the digital signature is valid and that the user has sufficient funds in their account. If the transaction is valid, it is added to the mempool, a list of unconfirmed transactions waiting to be included in a block.

The importance of digital signatures in the Bitcoin system cannot be overstated. Without digital signatures, it would be impossible to verify the ownership of a Bitcoin address or to ensure the authenticity of a transaction. Digital signatures provide a secure and efficient way to verify the identity of users and to protect against fraud and hacking.

It is worth noting that digital signatures are not perfect and are subject to certain limitations. For example, if a user's private key is compromised, an attacker could potentially sign fraudulent transactions on behalf of the user. This is why it is essential to protect private keys and to use secure storage solutions such as hardware wallets.

In summary, digital signatures are a crucial component of the Bitcoin system, providing a secure and efficient way to verify the ownership of Bitcoin addresses and to authorize transactions. While they are not perfect and are subject to certain limitations, digital signatures represent an essential tool for ensuring the integrity and authenticity of the Bitcoin network.

The role of inputs and outputs in a transaction

Bitcoin transactions involve the transfer of value between two parties. In order to initiate a transaction, the sender must identify the amount of Bitcoin they wish to send and the address of the recipient's wallet. These inputs are then used to create the transaction, which is broadcast to the Bitcoin network and eventually confirmed by miners.

Inputs and outputs are key components of Bitcoin transactions, as they determine the amount of Bitcoin being transferred and the destination of the funds. Inputs represent the funds being spent in a transaction, while outputs represent the destination of those funds.

Inputs

Inputs are the building blocks of a Bitcoin transaction. They represent the unspent outputs of previous transactions that are being spent in the current transaction. Each input is associated with a specific transaction output, which is identified by its transaction ID and output index. The amount of Bitcoin associated with each input is determined by the value of the output being spent.

When creating a transaction, the sender must specify the inputs that they wish to spend. This involves selecting one or more unspent outputs from their own wallet that have been received in previous transactions. The sum of the inputs selected must be greater than or equal to the amount being sent in the current transaction. Any excess value in the inputs will be returned to the sender's wallet as change.

Outputs

Outputs represent the destination of the funds being transferred in a Bitcoin transaction. Each output is associated with a specific address, which is a string of characters that identifies the recipient's wallet. The amount of Bitcoin associated with each output is specified by the sender when creating the transaction.

When a transaction is broadcast to the Bitcoin network, it is sent to all nodes on the network. Miners then verify the transaction and add it to a block in the blockchain. Once a transaction has been confirmed, the recipient can access the funds by spending the associated output in a future transaction.

Transaction Fees

In addition to inputs and outputs, Bitcoin transactions also include a transaction fee. This fee is paid to miners as an incentive for including the transaction in a block. The fee is determined by the size of the transaction in bytes and the level of demand for block space on the network.

Transaction fees are an important aspect of the Bitcoin system, as they ensure that miners have an incentive to process transactions in a timely manner. Without transaction fees, miners would have little motivation to include transactions in their blocks, as they would not receive any compensation for their efforts.

Conclusion

The use of inputs and outputs is a critical component of the Bitcoin transaction process. Inputs represent the funds being spent in a transaction, while outputs represent the destination of those funds. Understanding the role of inputs and outputs is essential for anyone looking to use Bitcoin for transactions or to develop applications on top of the Bitcoin protocol. Additionally, the inclusion of transaction fees helps to ensure the security and stability of the Bitcoin network by providing incentives for miners to process transactions.

Chapter 2: Validating Bitcoin Transactions

The role of nodes in validating transactions

In the Bitcoin system, nodes play a crucial role in validating transactions. Nodes are essentially computers or devices that run the Bitcoin software and participate in the network. When a transaction is created and broadcasted to the network, it needs to be validated by the nodes before it can be added to the blockchain.

Nodes are responsible for verifying that the transaction is valid, which means it meets certain criteria. Firstly, the transaction must be properly formatted according to the rules of the Bitcoin protocol. This includes ensuring that the transaction inputs and outputs are properly defined and that the transaction size does not exceed the maximum limit. Nodes also verify that the transaction has a valid digital signature, which ensures that the sender of the transaction is authorized to spend the funds.

To validate a transaction, a node checks the inputs to ensure that the sender has sufficient funds to cover the transaction amount. Nodes also check the previous transactions associated with these inputs to ensure that they were not already spent in a previous transaction. This process of verifying the transaction inputs is known as the

"UTXO" (Unspent Transaction Output) model, which is used in the Bitcoin system to keep track of the ownership of Bitcoin.

Once a node has verified a transaction, it will add it to its own mempool. The mempool is a list of unconfirmed transactions that have been validated by the node, but have not yet been included in a block. Nodes prioritize transactions in their mempool based on the transaction fee offered by the sender. Transactions with higher fees are given higher priority and are more likely to be included in the next block.

Nodes communicate with each other to ensure that all nodes in the network have the same view of the mempool and the blockchain. This process of consensus is critical to the security of the Bitcoin network, as it ensures that all nodes have a consistent view of the transaction history.

In summary, nodes play a crucial role in validating Bitcoin transactions by verifying their validity, adding them to the mempool, and communicating with other nodes to reach consensus on the state of the network. The importance of nodes in the Bitcoin system cannot be overstated, as they are essential to maintaining the integrity and security of the network.

The concept of a mempool and how it works

The mempool, short for memory pool, is an essential component of the Bitcoin network that plays a critical role in validating transactions. It is a data structure that stores all unconfirmed transactions that have been broadcasted to the network by users. Miners use the mempool to select transactions to include in the next block they mine.

The mempool is a dynamic structure that is constantly changing as new transactions are added and confirmed transactions are removed. When a user sends a transaction, it is broadcasted to the Bitcoin network and received by all nodes. Each node verifies the transaction to ensure that it meets the network's consensus rules, and if it does, the node adds the transaction to its mempool.

The mempool is essentially a waiting room for transactions. It's where they wait until a miner chooses to include them in a block. When a new block is mined, the transactions in the mempool that have the highest transaction fees attached to them are typically selected first by miners to include in the new block. This is because miners are incentivized to include transactions with higher fees because they receive those fees as a reward for mining the block.

In addition to transaction fees, the size of a transaction also plays a role in determining whether it will be included in the next block. Each block has a limited size, which means that only a certain number of transactions can be included in each block. Therefore, miners typically choose to include smaller transactions with lower data sizes over larger transactions with higher data sizes.

The mempool is an important part of the Bitcoin network because it ensures that all transactions are validated before they are added to the blockchain. This helps to prevent fraudulent transactions and ensures that the network remains secure and reliable. The mempool also helps to ensure that the network can handle a high volume of transactions by allowing miners to select transactions with higher fees and smaller data sizes, which allows them to mine blocks faster.

It is worth noting that transactions that are not included in a block after a certain period are removed from the mempool. This period varies depending on the node's configuration but typically ranges from a few hours to a few days. If a transaction is not included in a block within this period, it is considered expired and can be broadcasted again to the network.

In conclusion, the mempool is an essential component of the Bitcoin network that plays a crucial role in validating transactions. It is a dynamic data structure that stores all unconfirmed transactions and allows miners to select which transactions to include in the next block they mine. By understanding how the mempool works, users can better understand how their transactions are processed and how to ensure that their transactions are confirmed quickly.

The importance of transaction fees in the validation process

Transaction fees play a crucial role in the Bitcoin network, as they incentivize miners to include transactions in the blocks they create. Without transaction fees, miners would have little motivation to include transactions in the limited block space available. In this section, we will explore the importance of transaction fees in the validation process and how they impact the Bitcoin network.

Transaction Fees: An Overview

When a user sends a Bitcoin transaction, they have the option to include a transaction fee. This fee is paid to the miner who includes the transaction in a block, and it is considered an incentive to prioritize the transaction. Miners are free to choose which transactions to include in a block, and they will typically prioritize transactions that offer higher fees.

Transaction fees are measured in satoshis per byte (sats/byte), with one satoshi being the smallest unit of Bitcoin. The higher the fee, the more likely a miner is to include the transaction in their block. However, fees that are too low may result in the transaction being stuck in the mempool and never being included in a block.

The Importance of Transaction Fees

Transaction fees are important for two primary reasons: incentivizing miners and securing the network. First, transaction fees incentivize miners to include transactions in blocks, as they are paid for their efforts. If transaction fees were not included in the network, miners would have little incentive to prioritize transactions, as there would be no financial reward for doing so. This would result in longer wait times for users, as their transactions would not be confirmed as quickly.

Second, transaction fees help to secure the network by preventing spam attacks. Without transaction fees, it would be possible for an attacker to flood the network with a large number of low-value transactions, effectively clogging the network and making it difficult for legitimate transactions to be processed. By requiring a transaction fee for each transaction, the network is protected against such attacks.

The Impact of Transaction Fees on the Network

Transaction fees have a significant impact on the Bitcoin network, particularly in times of high transaction volume. When the network is congested and the demand for block space is high, transaction fees tend to increase as users compete to have their transactions included in the next block. This can result in high fees, which can make it difficult for some users to send Bitcoin transactions.

However, the impact of transaction fees on the network can be mitigated by the use of batching and Segregated Witness (SegWit). Batching involves combining multiple transactions into a single transaction, which reduces the number of transactions that need to be validated and included in a block. SegWit increases the effective block size by removing the signature data from a transaction, which reduces the size of the transaction and allows more transactions to be included in each block.

Conclusion

Transaction fees are an essential component of the Bitcoin network, as they incentivize miners to include transactions in blocks and help to secure the network against spam attacks. However, high transaction fees can make it difficult for some users to send Bitcoin transactions, particularly during times of high transaction volume. The impact of transaction fees on the network can be reduced through the use of batching and SegWit, which can increase the effective block size and reduce the number of transactions that need to be validated and included in each block.

Chapter 3: Mining Bitcoin Transactions
The role of miners in the system

In the Bitcoin system, miners play a critical role in ensuring that transactions are validated and added to the blockchain. Miners are essentially the backbone of the network, and they perform several functions that keep the system running smoothly.

At a high level, the role of miners in the system is to create new blocks, which are then added to the blockchain. Each block contains a set of transactions that have been validated and confirmed by the network, and miners are responsible for verifying the validity of each transaction in the block.

The process of mining a new block involves several steps. First, miners must receive a set of unconfirmed transactions from the network, which they will then include in the block they are trying to create. This set of unconfirmed transactions is known as the mempool, which we discussed in the previous chapter.

Once miners have selected which transactions they want to include in their block, they then compete to solve a complex mathematical puzzle. The first miner to solve the puzzle is then able to create the new block and add it to the blockchain.

The mining process is essential for maintaining the security and integrity of the Bitcoin network. Because each block is linked to the one that came before it, changing any transaction in a block would require a miner to solve the puzzle for every subsequent block. This makes it virtually impossible for an attacker to alter any previous transactions without expending an enormous amount of computational power.

The reward for successfully mining a new block is a certain number of newly-created bitcoins, which is known as the block reward. The block reward is halved every 210,000 blocks, which means that the amount of new bitcoins created through mining is gradually decreasing over time.

As the Bitcoin system has grown in popularity, the competition among miners to solve the mathematical puzzle and earn the block reward has become increasingly fierce. This has led to the development of specialized hardware, known as Application-Specific Integrated Circuits (ASICs), that are designed specifically for mining bitcoins. These ASICs are orders of magnitude more powerful than traditional CPUs or GPUs, and they have significantly increased the difficulty of mining new blocks.

Overall, miners play a crucial role in the Bitcoin system, and their efforts are essential for ensuring the security and reliability of the network. While the mining process can be complex and resource-intensive, it is an essential component of the Bitcoin ecosystem that helps to keep the system running smoothly.

The process of mining and creating new blocks

Bitcoin mining is a crucial process that maintains the integrity and security of the Bitcoin network. In this chapter, we will delve into the process of mining and creating new blocks in the Bitcoin system.

To understand how Bitcoin mining works, it is important to first understand what a block is. A block is a record of transactions that have been verified and added to the Bitcoin blockchain. Each block contains a set of transactions and a header that contains metadata about the block. The header includes the block's timestamp, a unique identifier called a "nonce," and a reference to the previous block in the chain.

The process of mining begins with the creation of a new block. Miners compete to solve a complex mathematical puzzle that is designed to require a significant amount of computational power. The puzzle is based on the SHA-256 algorithm and requires miners to find a hash value that meets a certain target difficulty level.

To solve the puzzle, miners use specialized hardware known as Application-Specific Integrated Circuits (ASICs) or Graphics Processing Units (GPUs). These devices are designed to perform large numbers of calculations quickly and efficiently, making them ideal for the intensive computational requirements of Bitcoin mining.

Once a miner solves the puzzle and finds a hash value that meets the target difficulty level, they broadcast their solution to the network. Other miners then verify the solution and, if it is correct, add the new block to the blockchain. The miner who solved the puzzle is rewarded with a block reward in the form of newly created bitcoins.

The block reward is currently 6.25 bitcoins, but it is halved every 210,000 blocks. This is known as the Bitcoin halving, and it is designed to ensure that the supply of bitcoins is limited and that their value remains stable over time.

In addition to the block reward, miners also receive transaction fees for including transactions in the block they create. Transaction fees are paid by users who want to have their transactions included in the next block, and they are essential for incentivizing miners to prioritize certain transactions over others.

Overall, the process of mining and creating new blocks is critical to the functioning of the Bitcoin system. It ensures that transactions are verified and added to the blockchain in a secure and decentralized manner, while also incentivizing miners to invest in the computational resources needed to maintain the network.

The concept of the block reward and its significance

The concept of the block reward is at the heart of the Bitcoin mining process. Essentially, this is the incentive that miners receive for dedicating their computational resources to secure the network and validate transactions. In this section, we will explore the details of the block reward and its significance in the Bitcoin system.

The Block Reward

When a miner successfully mines a new block, they are rewarded with a certain number of bitcoins. This reward is a key element in the Bitcoin protocol, as it incentivizes miners to invest significant computational resources into securing the network.

The current block reward is 6.25 bitcoins per block, a number that has been halved several times over the history of the network. Initially, the block reward was set at 50 bitcoins per block. This was reduced to 25 bitcoins per block in 2012, and then again to 12.5 bitcoins per block in 2016, before reaching the current level in 2020.

It's worth noting that the block reward is not the only source of income for miners. They also earn transaction fees, which are paid by users to have their transactions included in a block. However, the block reward is the primary source of income for miners, particularly in the early stages of the network when transaction fees were low.

Significance of the Block Reward

The block reward serves several important functions in the Bitcoin system. First and foremost, it provides an incentive for miners to dedicate their computational resources to secure the network. Without this incentive, it's unlikely that the network would have attracted the level of mining power it has today.

Secondly, the block reward serves as a mechanism for distributing new bitcoins into circulation. Since there is a fixed supply of bitcoins that can ever be created (21 million), the block reward is the only way that new bitcoins can be introduced into the system. As such, it plays a crucial role in controlling the rate of inflation in the Bitcoin economy.

Finally, the block reward has also been a key driver of the economic dynamics of the Bitcoin ecosystem. In the early days of the network, the block reward was a significant source of income for miners, and many individuals and companies invested heavily in mining operations. As the block reward has been reduced over time, the importance of transaction fees as a source of income for miners has grown, and the dynamics of the mining industry have evolved accordingly.

Conclusion

The block reward is a fundamental element of the Bitcoin protocol, serving as both an incentive for miners to secure the network and a mechanism for distributing new bitcoins into circulation. As such, it plays a crucial role in the economics of the Bitcoin ecosystem and is an important concept to understand for anyone looking to gain a deeper understanding of how the network functions.

Chapter 4: Securing the Bitcoin Network
The importance of network security in the Bitcoin system

One of the most critical aspects of the Bitcoin system is the security of its network. The decentralized and open nature of the system means that anyone can participate, which also means that there is a risk of malicious actors trying to disrupt or compromise the network. In this chapter, we will explore the importance of network security in the Bitcoin system and the measures that are taken to ensure its safety.

The need for network security

As a digital currency, Bitcoin is entirely reliant on its network for its existence and operation. Without a secure network, the Bitcoin system would be vulnerable to various types of attacks, including double-spending, 51% attacks, and Sybil attacks. Double-spending occurs when a user tries to spend the same Bitcoin twice, while a 51% attack is when a single entity controls more than 50% of the network's computing power, giving them the ability to manipulate transactions. Sybil attacks involve creating multiple fake identities to take over the network and control the flow of transactions.

To prevent these and other types of attacks, the Bitcoin network must be secured through a variety of means, including cryptography, consensus mechanisms, and network monitoring.

Cryptography in network security

Cryptography plays a crucial role in the security of the Bitcoin network. All transactions on the network are encrypted using public-key cryptography, which uses two keys, a public key, and a private key. The public key is used to encrypt the transaction, while the private key is used to decrypt it. This ensures that only the intended recipient can access the funds and prevents unauthorized access to the transaction.

Another cryptographic technique used in the Bitcoin system is hash functions. Hash functions are algorithms that convert data of any size into a fixed-length hash. These hashes are unique and cannot be reversed, which makes them useful in verifying the integrity of data. In the Bitcoin network, hash functions are used to create blocks, which are then added to the blockchain.

Consensus mechanisms

Consensus mechanisms are used in the Bitcoin network to ensure that all nodes agree on the state of the blockchain. There are several consensus mechanisms, including proof of work and proof of stake. In the proof of work mechanism, miners compete to solve complex mathematical problems to validate transactions and add blocks to the blockchain. In the proof of stake mechanism, users can stake their cryptocurrency to validate transactions and create new blocks.

Network monitoring

Network monitoring is also critical in ensuring the security of the Bitcoin network. Nodes on the network monitor for suspicious activity, such as double-spending or attempts to manipulate the blockchain. If suspicious activity is detected, nodes can reject the transaction or block the offending node from the network.

Conclusion

The security of the Bitcoin network is essential for the success and continued operation of the system. Cryptography, consensus mechanisms, and network monitoring all play a critical role in ensuring the security of the network and preventing malicious attacks. By understanding the importance of network security in the Bitcoin system, users and developers can work together to create a more robust and secure network for the future.

The role of cryptographic protocols in securing the system

Cryptographic protocols play a crucial role in securing the Bitcoin network. In order to understand how they work, it's important to first have a basic understanding of what cryptography is and how it's used in the context of digital security.

Cryptography is the practice of secure communication in the presence of third parties, also known as adversaries. In the digital world, cryptography is used to protect information such as data, messages, and transactions from being intercepted, altered, or stolen by unauthorized parties.

The Bitcoin network uses several cryptographic protocols to achieve security, some of which include:

1. Public key cryptography: This is a cryptographic system that uses two keys - a public key and a private key - to encrypt and decrypt messages. In the context of Bitcoin, each user has a unique public key that is used to receive payments and a private key that is used to authorize and sign transactions. Public key cryptography ensures that only the owner of a particular private key can authorize transactions involving their funds.

2. Hash functions: These are mathematical functions that convert data of any size into a fixed-size output. In the

context of Bitcoin, hash functions are used to generate digital fingerprints of transactions, which are then added to blocks on the blockchain. Hash functions ensure the integrity of the data being transmitted and make it difficult for attackers to alter or corrupt the information.

3. Digital signatures: Digital signatures are used to ensure that a particular transaction can only be authorized by the owner of the private key associated with the public key used to receive the payment. Digital signatures use a combination of hash functions and public key cryptography to create a unique signature for each transaction. This signature is then broadcast to the network along with the transaction itself and is used to verify that the transaction was authorized by the owner of the private key.

4. Proof of work: This is a cryptographic protocol used to secure the Bitcoin blockchain. In order for a block to be added to the blockchain, miners must perform a computationally intensive task that requires significant computational power and energy. This task is known as "mining" and is designed to be difficult and time-consuming to perform. The first miner to successfully mine a block is rewarded with a block reward, which is currently 6.25 BTC.

Together, these cryptographic protocols ensure the security and integrity of the Bitcoin network. By using a combination of public key cryptography, hash functions, digital signatures, and proof of work, the Bitcoin network is able to achieve a high degree of security and resistance to attacks. However, as with any security system, there is always the potential for vulnerabilities to be discovered and exploited, so it's important for the Bitcoin community to remain vigilant and continue to improve the network's security protocols over time.

The potential threats to the system and how they can be mitigated

Bitcoin's decentralized nature and its use of cryptographic protocols make it an inherently secure system. However, as with any complex system, there are potential threats that must be considered and mitigated to ensure the continued security and reliability of the network. In this section, we will discuss some of the potential threats to the Bitcoin system and explore how they can be mitigated.

1. 51% attacks:

A 51% attack occurs when a single entity or group of entities control more than 50% of the network's computing power. This would allow them to control the network and potentially double-spend transactions, effectively breaking the security and trust in the network. To mitigate this threat, the Bitcoin network relies on a proof-of-work consensus algorithm that requires miners to solve a cryptographic puzzle to validate transactions and add them to the blockchain. This makes it extremely difficult and costly for a single entity to control the majority of the network's computing power.

2. Sybil attacks:

Sybil attacks occur when an attacker creates multiple identities or nodes on the network to gain control or influence over the network. This could potentially allow them to manipulate transactions, create false identities, or censor transactions. To mitigate this threat, the Bitcoin network relies on a peer-to-peer network that relies on nodes to validate transactions and maintain the integrity of the network. Additionally, the network employs anti-sybil measures to prevent attackers from creating large numbers of fake identities.

3. Malicious software:

Malicious software, or malware, can infect computers and steal user's private keys or other sensitive information, which can lead to the loss of funds. To mitigate this threat, users should take care to only download software and wallets from trusted sources, regularly update their software, and use anti-virus software to prevent malware from infecting their devices.

4. Denial of service attacks:

Denial of service attacks occur when an attacker floods the network with traffic or requests, overwhelming the network and causing it to slow down or become unresponsive. To mitigate this threat, the network employs measures such as rate limiting and prioritizing transaction fees to prevent attackers from flooding the network.

5. Social engineering attacks:

Social engineering attacks involve tricking users into revealing their private keys or other sensitive information through techniques such as phishing or impersonation. To mitigate this threat, users should be educated on how to identify and avoid these types of attacks, and always verify the authenticity of any requests for sensitive information.

In conclusion, the Bitcoin network is inherently secure, but there are potential threats that must be considered and mitigated to ensure its continued security and reliability. By employing cryptographic protocols, anti-sybil measures, and other security measures, the network can remain secure and trustworthy for users around the world. However, users must also take responsibility for their own security by taking steps to protect their private keys and prevent malware or social engineering attacks.

Chapter 5: The Lightning Network
Overview of the Lightning Network

The Lightning Network is a second-layer protocol designed to solve the scalability problem of the Bitcoin network. It is a network of off-chain payment channels that enables instant and cheap transactions without the need for every transaction to be broadcasted and validated by the entire Bitcoin network. In this section, we will provide an overview of the Lightning Network and how it works.

What is the Lightning Network?

The Lightning Network is a decentralized network of payment channels built on top of the Bitcoin blockchain. It was proposed in 2015 by Joseph Poon and Thaddeus Dryja in a whitepaper titled "The Bitcoin Lightning Network: Scalable Off-Chain Instant Payments". The Lightning Network is designed to facilitate fast, cheap, and secure transactions by allowing users to open a payment channel with another party on the network.

Payment channels are essentially two-party agreements that allow users to conduct an unlimited number of transactions between themselves off the main blockchain. The Lightning Network leverages the security of the Bitcoin blockchain and the speed of off-chain transactions to create a network that can handle an enormous number of transactions per second.

How does the Lightning Network work?

The Lightning Network uses a smart contract system called Hashed Timelock Contracts (HTLCs) to facilitate payments between users. HTLCs are a type of smart contract that enables two parties to exchange funds without the need for trust between the parties or intermediaries. This is accomplished by using cryptographic proofs to ensure that funds can only be released to the correct recipient.

When two parties want to transact, they first create a payment channel between themselves on the Lightning Network. This is done by locking a certain amount of Bitcoin into a multi-signature address that requires the signatures of both parties to move funds. Once the channel is open, the parties can conduct an unlimited number of transactions between themselves without broadcasting them to the Bitcoin network.

The Lightning Network works by routing payments through a network of payment channels. If two parties want to transact with each other, but do not have a direct payment channel between them, they can use the Lightning Network to route the payment through other channels until it reaches the recipient. This is done using a process called onion routing, which is similar to the way the Tor network works.

Advantages of the Lightning Network

The Lightning Network has several advantages over traditional on-chain Bitcoin transactions.

Fast Transactions

Transactions on the Lightning Network are almost instant, as they are not subject to the confirmation times required by the Bitcoin network. Once the payment channel is open, users can transact as many times as they want, with each transaction taking only a fraction of a second to complete.

Low Transaction Fees

Transaction fees on the Lightning Network are significantly lower than on-chain Bitcoin transactions, as they are not subject to the fees required by the Bitcoin network. Users only pay a small fee to open and close payment channels.

Scalability

The Lightning Network is highly scalable and can handle an enormous number of transactions per second. This makes it an ideal solution for micropayments and other low-value transactions.

Privacy

The Lightning Network provides a high degree of privacy, as transactions are conducted off the main blockchain and are not visible to the public.

Conclusion

The Lightning Network is a promising solution to the scalability problem of the Bitcoin network. It provides a fast, cheap, and secure way to transact on the Bitcoin network and has the potential to revolutionize the way we use Bitcoin. While the Lightning Network is still in its early stages, it has already demonstrated its potential, and we can expect to see many exciting developments in the future.

The benefits and drawbacks of using the Lightning Network

The Lightning Network is a second layer solution built on top of the Bitcoin blockchain that aims to solve the issue of scalability and transaction speed. The network allows for instant and cheap micropayments that can be conducted without waiting for confirmations on the Bitcoin blockchain. While the Lightning Network brings significant benefits, it also comes with drawbacks that must be considered.

Benefits of the Lightning Network

1. Scalability: The Lightning Network has the potential to solve the scalability issue that Bitcoin currently faces. By allowing transactions to be conducted off-chain, the network can process a large number of transactions without putting a strain on the main blockchain.

2. Speed: Transactions on the Lightning Network are nearly instant, as they do not require confirmations on the blockchain. This makes the network an ideal solution for micropayments, which may not be feasible on the main blockchain due to the time it takes for transactions to be confirmed.

3. Lower fees: Since the Lightning Network transactions are conducted off-chain, they require much lower fees than transactions on the main blockchain. This

makes it an ideal solution for micropayments, which would be too expensive to conduct on the main blockchain.

4. Privacy: The Lightning Network offers a higher level of privacy than the main blockchain since transactions are conducted off-chain. This means that transactions are not visible to the entire network and can only be seen by the parties involved.

Drawbacks of the Lightning Network

1. Centralization: The Lightning Network is still in its early stages, and as a result, there are only a limited number of nodes that are currently running the network. This means that the network is still centralized, which can be a cause for concern for some users.

2. Liquidity: In order to conduct transactions on the Lightning Network, users must have liquidity on the network. This means that users must either open channels with other users or use a node that already has liquidity. This can be a barrier for some users who may not have enough liquidity on the network.

3. User experience: The Lightning Network is still in its early stages, and as a result, the user experience can be clunky and difficult to use. This can be a barrier for adoption since users may not be willing to use a network that is difficult to use.

4. Security: The Lightning Network is a relatively new technology, and as a result, there are still potential security risks that must be addressed. Since transactions on the Lightning Network are conducted off-chain, there is a risk of funds being lost or stolen if a node is compromised.

Conclusion

The Lightning Network is a promising solution to the scalability issue that Bitcoin currently faces. While it brings significant benefits such as scalability, speed, lower fees, and privacy, it also comes with drawbacks that must be considered. As the network continues to develop, it is likely that many of these drawbacks will be addressed, and the Lightning Network will become a widely adopted solution for micropayments and other transactions.

The potential for the Lightning Network to solve Bitcoin's scalability challenges

The Lightning Network is a layer two scaling solution for the Bitcoin network. It aims to solve the scalability challenges faced by Bitcoin by allowing users to conduct off-chain transactions without having to wait for confirmation on the main blockchain. The Lightning Network has been touted as a potential solution to Bitcoin's scalability challenges, but how effective is it?

The Lightning Network has several benefits that make it a promising solution to Bitcoin's scalability challenges. First, it allows for almost instant transactions, as they are conducted off-chain and do not require confirmation on the main blockchain. This means that users can conduct transactions in a matter of seconds, rather than minutes or even hours as is the case with on-chain transactions. This is particularly useful for small transactions, such as buying a cup of coffee, where waiting for confirmation on the main blockchain is impractical.

Second, the Lightning Network is designed to be highly scalable. Transactions can be routed through multiple channels, allowing for a high volume of transactions to be conducted simultaneously. This means that the Lightning

Network can handle a significantly higher volume of transactions than the Bitcoin network can on its own.

Third, the Lightning Network is designed to be highly secure. Transactions are conducted using multi-signature addresses, which require the consent of multiple parties before funds can be moved. This makes it difficult for malicious actors to steal funds or conduct fraudulent transactions.

Despite its benefits, the Lightning Network also has some drawbacks. One of the biggest concerns is that it is still a relatively new technology and has not been widely adopted yet. This means that there is a risk of technical issues and bugs that could potentially lead to loss of funds. Additionally, the Lightning Network requires users to open and maintain channels, which can be complicated and requires a certain level of technical expertise. This means that the Lightning Network may not be accessible to all users.

Another potential drawback of the Lightning Network is that it requires users to lock up their funds in channels in order to conduct off-chain transactions. This means that users may not be able to access their funds until the channels are closed, which can take several days. Additionally, if the other party in the channel goes offline or becomes unresponsive, users may not be able to access their funds until the channel is closed.

Despite these drawbacks, the Lightning Network has the potential to be a game-changer for Bitcoin's scalability challenges. By allowing for off-chain transactions, the Lightning Network can significantly increase the number of transactions that can be conducted on the Bitcoin network. This could potentially make Bitcoin a more viable option for everyday transactions, such as buying a cup of coffee or paying for goods and services online. Additionally, the Lightning Network could potentially reduce transaction fees on the Bitcoin network, making it more affordable for users to conduct transactions.

In conclusion, the Lightning Network has the potential to solve Bitcoin's scalability challenges by allowing for off-chain transactions that are fast, scalable, and secure. While it is still a relatively new technology and has some drawbacks, the Lightning Network is a promising solution that could make Bitcoin a more practical option for everyday transactions. However, it remains to be seen how widely adopted the Lightning Network will be and how effective it will be in practice.

Conclusion

The mechanics of Bitcoin transactions and how they contribute to the overall functioning of the system

Bitcoin is a decentralized digital currency that allows users to send and receive payments without the need for intermediaries such as banks or other financial institutions. The entire system is based on a peer-to-peer network, and every transaction is verified and recorded on a public ledger called the blockchain. In this section, we will explore the mechanics of Bitcoin transactions and their significance in contributing to the overall functioning of the system.

At a high level, a Bitcoin transaction involves the transfer of ownership of a certain amount of bitcoins from one address to another. An address is a unique identifier associated with a specific user or entity that holds bitcoins. When a transaction is initiated, the sender creates a message that contains the recipient's address, the amount of bitcoins to be transferred, and a digital signature that proves the sender's ownership of the bitcoins. This message is broadcast to the Bitcoin network, where it is validated by a network of nodes that check the digital signature and verify that the sender has sufficient funds to complete the transaction.

Once a transaction is validated, it is added to a pool of unconfirmed transactions called the mempool. Miners then compete to include these transactions in a new block that will be added to the blockchain. The miner who successfully mines a block is rewarded with newly minted bitcoins and transaction fees from the included transactions.

One of the key features of Bitcoin transactions is the use of cryptographic protocols to secure the network and prevent double-spending. Every transaction is signed with a digital signature that is unique to the sender and verified by the network. This ensures that the transaction cannot be altered or duplicated by anyone other than the sender.

Another important aspect of Bitcoin transactions is their irreversible nature. Once a transaction is confirmed and added to the blockchain, it becomes a permanent part of the ledger and cannot be undone. This feature provides an added layer of security and makes it difficult for fraudulent transactions to occur.

Bitcoin transactions also offer a high degree of privacy and anonymity, as users can create new addresses for each transaction and are not required to provide personal information. However, it is important to note that transactions are still recorded on the public blockchain, which can be used to track the movement of bitcoins.

In summary, Bitcoin transactions are a critical component of the Bitcoin system, enabling the transfer of value between users without the need for intermediaries. These transactions are secured by cryptographic protocols and are irreversible once confirmed and added to the blockchain. By understanding the mechanics of Bitcoin transactions, we gain insight into how the overall system functions and the benefits it offers in terms of privacy, security, and decentralization.

The challenges facing the Bitcoin system and potential solutions, such as the Lightning Network

Bitcoin has revolutionized the way we think about money and the financial system. Its decentralized nature, high level of security, and transparency have attracted a significant following since its inception. However, as with any new technology, there are challenges to overcome, and potential solutions to explore. In this section, we will discuss the challenges facing the Bitcoin system and potential solutions, such as the Lightning Network.

One of the most significant challenges facing Bitcoin is scalability. As more people use the system, the number of transactions increases, and the network becomes congested, leading to slower transaction times and higher fees. This is a significant problem for Bitcoin's mass adoption, as slow and expensive transactions are not user-friendly. Fortunately, several potential solutions exist.

One of the most promising solutions to Bitcoin's scalability challenge is the Lightning Network. The Lightning Network is a second-layer scaling solution that enables faster and cheaper transactions. It works by creating a network of payment channels between users. Users can transact with each other directly, without having to go through the main blockchain. This reduces the load on the blockchain and enables faster and cheaper transactions.

Another solution that has been proposed is increasing the block size limit. The block size limit is currently set at 1 MB, which limits the number of transactions that can be processed at any given time. Increasing the block size limit would allow more transactions to be processed per block, reducing congestion and improving transaction times. However, increasing the block size limit also increases the size of the blockchain, making it more challenging to run a node and increasing the centralization of the system.

Another potential solution to Bitcoin's scalability challenge is the use of sidechains. Sidechains are separate blockchains that are attached to the main Bitcoin blockchain. They enable users to transact with each other directly, without having to go through the main blockchain. This reduces the load on the main blockchain and enables faster and cheaper transactions. However, sidechains require a significant amount of development work, and their security is not yet well understood.

Another challenge facing Bitcoin is its energy consumption. Bitcoin mining requires a significant amount of energy, which has led to concerns about its impact on the environment. While some argue that Bitcoin's energy consumption is necessary to ensure the security of the network, others believe that more energy-efficient mining methods could be developed.

One potential solution to Bitcoin's energy consumption challenge is the use of renewable energy. Several Bitcoin mining companies have already started using renewable energy sources, such as solar and wind power, to power their mining operations. Additionally, new mining methods, such as Proof of Stake, are being developed that require significantly less energy than traditional Proof of Work mining.

In conclusion, Bitcoin has the potential to revolutionize the financial system. Its decentralized nature, high level of security, and transparency make it an attractive option for individuals and businesses alike. However, as with any new technology, there are challenges to overcome. The Lightning Network, increasing the block size limit, and the use of sidechains are all potential solutions to Bitcoin's scalability challenge. Renewable energy and new mining methods, such as Proof of Stake, are potential solutions to Bitcoin's energy consumption challenge. As the Bitcoin ecosystem continues to evolve, it is essential to address these challenges to ensure the long-term viability of the system.

The potential for further developments in the Bitcoin system to improve transaction speed and scalability

The Bitcoin system has come a long way since its inception, but there are still challenges that need to be addressed. One of the most pressing challenges is scalability. The current block size limit of 1 MB is not sufficient to accommodate the growing number of transactions on the network. As a result, transaction fees have skyrocketed, making it difficult for users to use Bitcoin for small transactions.

However, there are several potential solutions to this problem. One of the most promising is the Lightning Network, which we discussed earlier in this book. The Lightning Network enables fast, low-cost transactions by allowing users to create payment channels between themselves. These channels can be used to conduct multiple transactions without having to broadcast each one to the entire network, which reduces congestion on the main blockchain.

Another potential solution to the scalability problem is the implementation of the Schnorr signature algorithm. This algorithm enables the aggregation of multiple signatures into a single signature, which reduces the size of transactions and therefore increases the number of transactions that can fit into a block.

In addition to scalability, there are other challenges facing the Bitcoin system, such as security and privacy concerns. While the Bitcoin system is generally considered secure, there have been several high-profile hacks and thefts over the years, which highlight the need for continued vigilance and innovation in the realm of security.

One potential solution to security concerns is the implementation of multi-signature addresses, which require multiple signatures to authorize a transaction. This makes it more difficult for hackers to steal funds, as they would need access to multiple private keys.

Privacy is another area of concern in the Bitcoin system, as all transactions are recorded on the public blockchain. While the blockchain is pseudonymous, meaning that transactions are not linked to a user's real identity, there are still concerns about the privacy implications of having all transactions recorded in a public ledger.

One potential solution to this problem is the implementation of privacy-focused technologies such as zero-knowledge proofs and ring signatures. These technologies enable users to transact on the blockchain without revealing their identities or the amount of Bitcoin they are transacting.

In conclusion, while the Bitcoin system has made significant progress in recent years, there are still challenges that need to be addressed. Scalability, security, and privacy are among the most pressing concerns facing the system, but there are potential solutions that can help overcome these challenges. As the Bitcoin system continues to evolve, it is likely that we will see further developments that improve transaction speed and scalability, as well as enhance security and privacy. The future of Bitcoin is bright, and it will be interesting to see how the system develops in the years to come.

THE END

Key Terms and Definitions

To help you better understand the language and concepts related to aging and older adults, below you will find a list of key terms and their definitions.

1. Bitcoin: A decentralized digital currency that operates on a peer-to-peer network and uses cryptography for security.

2. Blockchain: A digital ledger that records transactions made in Bitcoin or other cryptocurrencies.

3. Cryptography: The practice of using codes and ciphers to secure communication.

4. Digital Signature: A mathematical technique used to verify the authenticity of digital messages or documents.

5. Mining: The process of adding new transactions to the blockchain and verifying their authenticity by solving complex mathematical puzzles.

6. Mempool: A list of unconfirmed transactions waiting to be processed and added to the blockchain.

7. Nodes: Computers connected to the Bitcoin network that participate in the validation and propagation of transactions.

8. Transaction: A transfer of Bitcoin or other cryptocurrency from one address to another.

9. Input: The amount of Bitcoin being sent in a transaction.

10. Output: The destination address for the Bitcoin being sent in a transaction.

11. Wallet: A software program or device used to store and manage Bitcoin and other cryptocurrencies.

12. Lightning Network: A second-layer protocol built on top of the Bitcoin blockchain that aims to improve transaction speed and scalability.

Supporting Materials
Bitcoin Whitepaper

According to the original Bitcoin whitepaper (https://bitcoin.org/bitcoin.pdf) that was authored by Satoshi Nakamoto and titled "Bitcoin: A Peer-to-Peer Electronic Cash System.", here are the page numbers that could be covered in each book:

Book 1/3:

Introduction: Pages 1-2

Chapter 1: "Introduction" section on Page 1

Chapter 2: "Transactions" section on Pages 2-4

Chapter 3: "Timestamp Server" section on Pages 4-5

Chapter 4: "Proof-of-Work" section on Pages 5-7

Chapter 5: "Network" section on Pages 7-8

Conclusion: Pages 8-9

Book 2/3:

Introduction: Pages 1-2

Chapter 1: "Introduction" section on Page 1

Chapter 2: "The Economics of Bitcoin" section on Pages 2-3

Chapter 3: "Bitcoin and Financial Inclusion" section on Pages 3-4

Chapter 4: "Bitcoin and Social Implications" section on Pages 4-6

Chapter 5: "Bitcoin and Income Inequality" section on Pages 6-7

Conclusion: Pages 8-9

Book 3/3:

Introduction: Pages 1-2

Chapter 1: "Introduction" section on Page 1

Chapter 2: "Future Directions" section on Pages 2-3

Chapter 3: "Regulatory Landscape" section on Pages 3-4

Chapter 4: "Potential Applications" section on Pages 4-5

Chapter 5: "Bitcoin and the Environment" section on Pages 5-6

Conclusion: Pages 8-9

Potential References

Introduction

Nakamoto, S. (2008). Bitcoin: A Peer-to-Peer Electronic Cash System.

Chapter 1

Overview of the Bitcoin System: Antonopoulos, A. M. (2014). Mastering Bitcoin: Unlocking Digital Cryptocurrencies. O'Reilly Media, Inc.

Chapter 2

Cryptographic Protocols in Bitcoin: Narayanan, A., Bonneau, J., Felten, E., Miller, A., & Goldfeder, S. (2016). Bitcoin and Cryptocurrency Technologies: A Comprehensive Introduction. Princeton University Press.

Introduction:

- Antonopoulos, A. M. (2014). Mastering Bitcoin: Unlocking Digital Cryptocurrencies. O'Reilly Media, Inc.

Chapter 1: Creating Bitcoin Transactions

- Narayanan, A., Bonneau, J., Felten, E., Miller, A., & Goldfeder, S. (2016). Bitcoin and Cryptocurrency Technologies: A Comprehensive Introduction. Princeton University Press.

- Antonopoulos, A. M. (2014). Mastering Bitcoin: Unlocking Digital Cryptocurrencies. O'Reilly Media, Inc.

Chapter 2: Validating Bitcoin Transactions

- Narayanan, A., Bonneau, J., Felten, E., Miller, A., & Goldfeder, S. (2016). Bitcoin and Cryptocurrency Technologies: A Comprehensive Introduction. Princeton University Press.
- Antonopoulos, A. M. (2014). Mastering Bitcoin: Unlocking Digital Cryptocurrencies. O'Reilly Media, Inc.

Chapter 3: Mining Bitcoin Transactions

- Narayanan, A., Bonneau, J., Felten, E., Miller, A., & Goldfeder, S. (2016). Bitcoin and Cryptocurrency Technologies: A Comprehensive Introduction. Princeton University Press.
- Antonopoulos, A. M. (2014). Mastering Bitcoin: Unlocking Digital Cryptocurrencies. O'Reilly Media, Inc.

Chapter 4: Securing the Bitcoin Network

- Narayanan, A., Bonneau, J., Felten, E., Miller, A., & Goldfeder, S. (2016). Bitcoin and Cryptocurrency Technologies: A Comprehensive Introduction. Princeton University Press.
- Antonopoulos, A. M. (2014). Mastering Bitcoin: Unlocking Digital Cryptocurrencies. O'Reilly Media, Inc.

Chapter 5: The Lightning Network

- Poon, J., & Dryja, T. (2016). The Bitcoin Lightning Network: Scalable Off-Chain Instant Payments. White Paper, 14(5).

- Narayanan, A., Bonneau, J., Felten, E., Miller, A., & Goldfeder, S. (2016). Bitcoin and Cryptocurrency Technologies: A Comprehensive Introduction. Princeton University Press.

Conclusion

- Antonopoulos, A. M. (2014). Mastering Bitcoin: Unlocking Digital Cryptocurrencies. O'Reilly Media, Inc.
- Narayanan, A., Bonneau, J., Felten, E., Miller, A., & Goldfeder, S. (2016). Bitcoin and Cryptocurrency Technologies: A Comprehensive Introduction. Princeton University Press.

www.ingramcontent.com/pod-product-compliance
Lightning Source LLC
LaVergne TN
LVHW012127070526
838202LV00056B/5903